THE DEVIL'S WORKSHOP

The Devil's Workshop

FIRST EDITION

Printed in the United States of America

ISBN 978-1-7348167-8-5

DESIGN ≈ SEVY PEREZ

Text in Brandon Grotesque & Adobe Caslon Pro

This book is published by the

Cleveland State University Poetry Center

csupoetrycenter.com

2121 Euclid Avenue, Cleveland, Ohio 44115-2214

and is distributed by

SPD / Small Press Distribution, Inc.

spdbooks.org

1341 Seventh Street Berkeley, California 94710-1409

a CATALOG RECORD *for this* TITLE *is*

AVAILABLE *from the* LIBRARY OF CONGRESS

THE DEVIL'S WORKSHOP

XAVIER CAVAZOS

IN ORDER OF APPEARANCE

Addiction
Assault
Love

Demons
Sloth
Divorce
Abandonment
Death

Abuse
Curanderismo
Sodomy
Forgiveness
Lust
Gluttony
Murder
Drunkenness

Greed
Wrath
Shame
Envy
Deliverance
Pride
Democracy
Crime

Punish-
Ment
Sal-
Va-
Tio-
N

for
Wendy Barnes

for

the addicted

(hope in recovery)

"Language is not an animal you can train."
—Eduardo C. Corral

CONTENTS

I was cleaning

The Top

of the ceiling

like a caged orangutan.
The poison coming out of me.

Each brown hair on my body
blown flat like Armageddon trees from all the sweat.

I was cleaning the black stains
that floated

to the top of the white walls from my bubble-clubbed glass
pipe.

Hands black as the rim
of my mouth after rubbing the burnt belly of the bowl.

She locked herself
in the bathroom for hours—tried to get the insects

under her skin to come out & forward into the world
of the dead.

I laughed
as her face fell onto the floor like all of her dreams,

& her mother tried to have me arrested—

no law against pick a face
                                        off.

                                        Together
we were part of something whole.

We'd smile at each other,
 my black mouth

          and hands, her face
          on the floor.

My Father

the Golden Eagle

made arrows from broad wings.
    A tall light-brown raptor with many nests.

My father, the bird of prey—
    "I love you" was always a hundred-dollar bill

of speedbump-hotwired heartbeat & shrugs in the morning.
    "I'm sorry Mijo," he would say. The electricity bill lost

for ten years & a house kept warm
    from a small fire burning on the stove.

Patience holds the mold on the wall. Maybe we were hares,
    rabbits, marmots, and ground squirrels

                    to him. Oh, the tricks
    he played in the air—

his voice a flame-in-fever on
    the cliff he was clinging to.

A chirp, a seeir, a pssa, a skonk, a honk, a wonk,
    a hiss, but usually a cluck

on a ledge—

my father's voice.

My father, good eagle that he was
thought all his children could soar—

that all of us would have a strong hallux claw—
my weapon of choice. So I dove with him—

hit after hit—my feather tracts erect.
Eyes bugged & ready to pluck,

or grab, any white-shiny-thing
from the carpet fuzz.

From the porch where my

Father's Body

was wrapped in a sestina

My sixty-two-year-old daddy died in a crack house,
fallen over like a Vietnam vet, a First Infantry Airborne soldier
with a University of Washington Husky purple & gold
pride sweatshirt ripped from his belly-button chest
center-bottom all the way up to his snug-neck-tip-top
collar & tossed eternally to his side.

My daddy died with lots of scavengers at his side.
No stem cell research going on in that house,
mercenaries shuffling through a dead man's top
trouser pocket, fueled from the fumes of a soldier's
Chore Boy-Brillo pushed down the glass stem with a chest
flush with ash desperate from a house of war-addict gold.

My sixty-two-year-old daddy, dead like a gold
prayer, an eternal goodness. My daddy died lying side
down, right cheek & Chicano shoulder-chest
shoved hard onto a wilted-up green linoleum. The house
was trampled with wet leaves & caked mudprints of soldiers
holding the final resting place of my father like a swirling top.

The sizzle of the burnt-rock sound in the glass-stem top
made me more violent than any TV soldier after blood & gold.
Somebody told me my daddy died long before he was a soldier,
long before I followed him over to the crack-pledge-of-allegiance side,
that break-glass, scream, tie-up, smash & broken-face house
with lots of crackhead friends with Aztec-calendar chest

tattoos. My daddy was the sun, always burned his chest
with lies. He was addicted to the sound of losing dollars on top
of dollars for fucks, or a crisp-crackling sound in a hollow house,
bread broken over a spoon & glass jar flame, an open fire of soul & gold.
Farewell, father, as you listened to the old record playing from the far side
of the Earth's ozone-tropopause-station for cracked-amigo soldiers.

My daddy was a full-of-disaster amigo-amigo soldier,
could-get-a-cheap-car-in-repo, cavalier kind of guy, would puff his chest
in church & smile, never could get the rock out of his mouth-side,
even when he ran for people's-mayor, was the top
choice & won because he was Hispanic-news-pho-soup-Vietnam-gold.
White Center & the family left waiting for him in his 18th Ave. S.W. house.

Time to say goodbye & salute the broken-curtain home of my fallen father solider.
Time to enter & lock the golden room of god's-great-grace-forgiveness chest.
Time to top a farewell. Time & a little boy kicks a long-cast shadow outside.

Lo.

The Devil's Workshop

1.

The beauty of a burning bowl of ice or shooting syringe is a bloody plume field-dress of planetarium-crystallized bandages on a junkie-plantation battlefield—soft, dense, white-smoke fills inside a head like a hot-air balloon, graceful, ready to lift off the edge of this earth.

The release of smoke from lung is a slow, full-billow of the hit coming out of warm mouth—a birth—a new crowning head.

Whispers "sharpshooter Shangri-La-Shanghai" alert, not erect. An eyes-bugged platoon.

The Devil's Workshop

1.

Awake. Can't shit. Crusted

saliva. Crusted black stains on

the hand, the lip. Fuck. Fucked

up. Big chunks of coagulated

blood and dope in the spoon.

The dope, a drowned

swimmer.   Need to clean

the hit—rinse it, so to speak.

Fresh cotton

and wet it a bit.

          Liquid in the spoon.

                    Tip of

the plunger off.

Carefully. Once the tip

of the

p-

l-

u-

n-

g-

e-

r

is off,

use it to wiggle

the coagulated blood—shake it

away from reality. The hit

up (parchment)

up (parchment)

up (parchment)

into the syringe through a new

cotton—a new carnival—a

Ferris wheel ride—a demolition

derby—the animal barn—a

blue ribbon award.

Push

the

hit

of dope directly into

blood. A sunny day

bankruptcy—ashtray of gold—

a mother's warm face. The

needle registering in the arm is a

Mona Lisa—I am child before

the wound when the tip of the

needle enters my vein and there

is a perfect stream of blood—a

mushrooming red plume. The

register is a rolling upward billow

of red, a billowing flame.

A dollop of

blood—a red running fox.

Then

W

H

A

M.

Taller Del Diablos. 29

Clinton Street

NYC, NY

A Bremerton ferry dips behind an island. My dogs
are chasing me and all my dreams collapse

in a shooting gallery. Gulls sing the sky and the sun,
setting like my marriage, lets the tide go out.

I'm running down a street in New York City.
Everything around me is concrete and skyscraper,

junkie elite and reefer ragtime.
I'm running and I come to a river.

I see my two dogs, Lucy and Slim.
They're drowning in the current

and in the current consumption
of my arm, they die.

When I walk home after the funeral,
my arm is glowing.

The street vendors call me by my name.
They say, "Junkie, junkie, where are your dogs?"

"Junkie, junkie, where is your wife, the one with a pink scarf?"
"Junkie, junkie," as they push their carts.

The ocean cracks and fish disappear. A brown one,
beautiful as my mother, flops to the ocean shore.

I try to cook the fish for nourishment
but feel my ribs getting warm.

When I look in the mirror
I see a volcano has formed at my side

and lava is running from my ears.
I take a white towel to wipe my head

and rub my father's death
ashes all over my face.

The burnt fish I carry in my pocket comes alive.
The fish flops and flops and my mother is smiling

in the picture I hold. Here I go,
Mom, on the back of a squirrel,

holding an ear, I'm dressed in green.
Over the moon, Mom, I am flying up like my love for you,

floating into stars, I am taking all my love
for you with me,

all the way with me, over the moon,
but my conscience leaps out before me like

a bowl of dog food. My dogs lick the bowl clean.
They pant, their saliva strong, and small crumbs sparkle

the kitchen floor like hope or a marriage.
My shoulders ache from their teeth, ache from the walks,

the garbage can, the rats and the *ring-cling-clink*
sound of their dog tags wake me in my sleep.

Ring-cling-clink, ring-
cling-clink.

Hello, my name is…
Have you seen my two dogs?

They're pit bulls, brindle, and look like twins.
I dropped them off here last week.

You said my soul would live if I dropped them off.
You said I would be able to breathe, sleep, and eat.

You said I wouldn't come back looking for them
the way I did the Lynda Diva-Go-Cart Café,

but lately the weather is all rain, hot and sour like your words
and I run from street to corner to garbage to toilet

to rainbow to star, looking for all of them.
The walls around me are red and constant

with their blood and broken vows. The air I breathe
is filled with no-barking.

Ring-cling-clink, ring-cling-clink, cling-clink, cling-clink, clink.
This river leads straight to hell, everyone is segregated:

Blacks on one side, whites on the other,
Mexicans behind a fence. Magnolias blossom as I glide past the East

Indians and Pakistanis in the rain. One tree breaks
and a cottage full of relatives crashes to the river bank.

They run out with my diaper in hand and save me before
I sink. The raft I was on is moving without my help

and daisies appear under my feet. Blacks on the left.
Browns on the right. Yellows under the dirt.

Whites above the cliff. Reds wherever they want to go.
The river is raging linden, butterflies, ants, moss, and goat.

The river is raging cows, horses, good meat, sour meat, spiders, and mites.
The river is raging needles, cotton, spoons, blood, and swabs.

The river is raging cantaloupe, watermelon, rhubarb, and lemonade.
The river is raging houses, banks, lovers, cheats, and death.

The river is raging, and calling, and the cunning devil tempted me.
For three thousand days and nights he threw

beautiful women at my feet. The laughter
of their children froze me like a snake

at the edge of a campsite.
He said, "Do you believe in me?" and I stood

in the wind of the shine and the ocean shore
and stared at the clouds and the sand and the air,

and dolphins leaped before me and I saw eels and octopi
and mermaids. He placed beautiful forest trees at my side

and gold in front of my eyes. He said, "This could be yours,
do you believe in me?" and in the cold hotel rooms

with families-of-the-frozen, we sat like disciples around the offering
table. We'd bow our heads and pray for nourishment.

We'd say "Jesus, Lucifer, Luke,"
and the food would fall from the ceiling of heaven

and the nourishment was so ugly. It gleamed or
glowed like the holes in our arms as we broke bread.

And we'd give thanks and bow our heads again,
and pray, and we'd say "Jesus, Lucifer,"

and take ice from the freezer and rub
our arms with it until the ice melted away.

And we'd give thanks again,
and we'd pray and we'd say "Jesus!"

And the babies of the mothers would cry
on the empty beds, in the cold hotel rooms.

And we'd laugh and we'd get high,
and we'd give thanks and we'd say,

"Jesus, Luke, Lucifer,
amen."

Harrowing of Hell

666.

My mom took my face, a failed

rocket, lifted me off the floor and asked,

Do you believe in the Holy Spirit, the holy Catholic Church, the communion of saints?

And if you do, tell me where it hurts Mijo, tell

me. I held my hand to the

right side of my face, a torpedo net of

electricity drilling a hole through my

tooth and into my brain.

Or was it the insects scratching

rough through my cracked-out topical

skin injection?

"Right here, Mom," I said and

held my hand

to my face

My mother

then   squared

herself like a linebacker.

She said to keep my eyes locked

on hers. My tongue-tied tooth, my

tomfoolery toilet-flush hotel room, my

tea-kettle blood mist.

My mother

then clapped her hands

and rubbed them up

and down—a small fire kindled around

us.   She placed one hand

in the air—a radio tower,

a transmitter from this

to that,

and the other hand

on my cheek

where the dying tooth was—

current to my soul and said,

Demon Face Jezebel, Bathsheba!

and in tongues spoke,

Shubadha,

Nicarra,

Ruskadha.

My mother clapped her hands

again and said,

Baal, I command you with eyes

aflame

with fire

and feet of fine brass,

I command the

minions of the tribe

of the Spirit of Perversion,

and unto the Angel

of the Church in

the Synagogue of Satan

I command you to

leave *now.*

And a fire—my face a pit of

flames.

Spirits of the Tribe of Multi-Perversions. And

instantly prophetess

Jezebel opened her mouth to

me like a flower blooming.

My mother

put her hand over my mouth

and said,

Let the living say out loud glory to the

highest! *And in*

the throne room of God, it is! Halleluiahs

The whimpering spirits

spit back yellow saliva

at my mom

and Baal, in a low rumble said,

"Thou aren't worthy,

O woman, to receive glory and honor

and power. Ahoy."

On the ridge,

a loud audible blasphemy!—thunder

crack, was heard. "Blasphemy!—

thunder crack.

Blasphemy—

thunder crack!" And the sky

split open

like two legs

on a bed—a river of blood and

diamonds rushing over me.

Sweet Jesus, Holy

Judas—Spirit of Betrayal and Shame,

Queens of Heaven,

Sweet Mary may I,

My mother shook me

and said, *Baal! Fugitives into the wilderness I*

command you now, the

communion of saints,

menstruation of the soul,

the forgiveness

of sins, merge of mercy,

the resurrection of the

body, mango and mangrove in the man-hole.

Manslaughter

and life everlasting. I command you

now. Malign like a dead mallard.

"Blasphemy!—thunder crack.

Blasphemy!—thunder crack."

The she-wolf-demon spirit

whimpered, and rebuked. "Lo the holy

believe in the church

I the unholy in

you.

A banquet of

loss and open

sores—a legion of sorrow.

Spirit of Perversion,

and Bondage—

Beelzebub, am I only."

The Devil's Workshop

1.

Buckled over like a puking college kid. My tooth is dying. My tooth is an abused kid—a burning-black-bowl of ice. I'd shower my tooth in the morning, make out with mouths that had no mothers late in the afternoon—bat mitzvahed base hit mouths that swallowed el leche. French-kiss mouths—mouths that wouldn't shut up—glee club kind of mouths. Pitch Perfect One, Two, and Three kind of mouths. Snowball, sodomy, and snuff—mouths,

soft, dense, opening mouths. Jesus mouths—holy mother of Mary mouths—crucified mouths—whipped slave-ship Snoop Dogg mouths.

Taller Del Diablos.

The Devil's Workshop

1.

Coke hits swirl in the mouth's lip—a graceful figure-eight, eight-ball. An Apolo Ohno speed-ball skater—petite, dazzling as the hit spins in the blood and rushes to the

C

R

O

T

C

H.

Coke hits are the most dangerous—a wild tiger. If the hit is too big, too extra-large or strong, it will earthquake a person—a hanged-man or dead girl in bed. The mind's eye in parallax, shaking the whole body—a papier-mâché of brain rattle, bathroom, and breath.

From a Capitol Hill sidewalk after seeing

Dael Orlandersmith

all the way out in Washington

Back in Brooklyn we used broken Spanish to communicate between two,
sometimes three, four, maybe five different countries all flipped upside

down, standing on their own ABCs. However, on the Lower East Side of Manhattan,
a bag of C = coke. No joke. D = dope, dope. A bag of C & D

cost a dub, a chubby-hub-weekend-chug, a real-dude-dud-club.
Back in Brooklyn we were two budding amigos, brown & Black.

Two blossoming-the-spring-green-in-New York kind of daisies,
you with plays & me my subway rants

that took a back seat to my dimes blooming
into bundles & bundles were twelve dimes for the price of nine.

We would keep entire boroughs at bay, the way we'd play with words
& words became worlds & Verrazzano & Staten Island were the points

of intersection. Dig the reference. Avenue B & Clinton,
the mean, median & mode. Eighth Avenue & 33rd where things

broke down. "Flip, subtract, divide, motherfucker," I would scream.
Last time I saw you, Dael, I was running a block behind you,

your hair as recognizable as my mother's face.
All points that mattered erased or stolen like the bag in my hand,

and lined me up another astro-nut-lunar-orbit,
another fellow who-sold-my-soul-for-dope-romp-stomp.

I said what I need from you, Dael, is an L.E.S. love-song.
A Nuyorican hug. A back to health real-deal-Dael-comrade

who can catch me in mid-stride, alter my trajectory. A real-deal-Dael
who can absorb this speed, this pace. Last time I saw you, Dael, my back was bent

& bursting like a baby dropped & fried in a pan & what motherfucking
you must have thought as I flew past you, all the way out here in Seattle,

& you jumped back like I was cockroach gang, a *Yellowman*,
a donkey-ass-backward orb, as I tumbled eighteen thousand miles per hour.

What could you have thought, other than Oh-my-fucking-god,
there goes my fallen brother, a massive tumbling sphere,

Beauty's Daughter. Oh-my-god, a bright burning rock,
a Nuyorican orbiting-comet,

Oh-my, this bursting-flame,
this racing *Monster*,

Oh, this
beast.

Harrowing of Hell
// 666. //

My mother said,

I can see you, your spirit you,

bondage, who has been locked in a room or cell for seven-hundred-thousand years.

// *The door is locked,* //

// *can you see the door?* //

// "No," I answered, //

// "it's dark." //

// *Stay locked*

onto my eyes //

no matter what.

                    I need you

to look for a key.

                    It's there in the // cell. //

Find it

                    and   let   yourself

/ / / / / / / / / / / /   *out.*   / / / / / / / / / / / /

/ /

I was in dreamland—

                    I could feel my body

moving—squint-eyed and hollow and

near a staircase was a songbird in

somersault with my soul.

But I could also see

the reflection of myself

on my mother's eyeball.

In the reflection,

a Spanish conquistador

on a horse

with a sword and my mother

on a horse

with a sword

I kept thinking horse, thinking smack,

thinking smack the horse.

I wanted more smack.

I saw Mary

Magdalen

with

beads

and

jewels

like

a

needle

and a purple flowing

gown

riding on a beast

with four heads

and seven horns. I saw the angel

from the church of Philadelphia.

I turned

quickly to see if the beast and angel

were behind me—

shears of a sheep-run and shuddering.

I saw

nothing, only my mother's

bookshelf and hanging pictures

on the wall. A low

voice said slow, "The holy

believe in the church.

I the unholy in you.

Holy

the

church will fall."

"Who is speaking?"

I

asked my mom.

Stay locked onto my eyes. My mom

pressed her Bible onto my chest, and

continued.

Beelzebub,

Spirit of Lust, you are at the marriage

supper of the lamb—Halleluiah!

"Blasphemy!—

thunder crack.

Blasphemy!"

I

command you, with

the blood of the lamb,

the seven spirits of God, and with the seven

stars.

"Mother!" I shouted,

and I heard trumpets.

"What's happening?"

I needed to vomit,

I let out a howl. The force of

my breath

a concussion. My back

completely bent, my head cocked

like a gun

and I let out

a thick moan

that filled the small

living room corners

to the ceiling and out

of the house's roof—a wolf

in the wilderness,

aflame.

Harrowing of Hell

666.

My teeth dying, crumpling like a cup of melting ice. In the kitchen my mom circled-back and hard-boiled around me. Her hardened face entered from another entrance into the dining room. She began blessing with the four corners of the room, her arms tossing holy oil to counter my harlotry tongue. Her voice haruspex—in the name of the Father—a harvesting of souls on Canterbury Lane.

Her tongue, heavy and strong, sharp even, (kill, kill-deer, kidney, kilogram) as they pinned my arms to the kitchen table. I wanted to get up and run, correr, correr, correr, but I couldn't—killer bee, killer whale. She sprinkled oil in the air. Her words and ointment burned the spirits from my libidinous skin—Khan, kibosh

or kick? I could hear the spirits
whimpering like beaten dogs—
a killing, a kill-joy.

I finally broke

free from the verbal binding at the table and jumped up. "Mom, madre, manteca!" I shouted.

An electrical shock hit my mouth like jumpstart. The shock funneled into my dying tooth and dropped me to my knees—dewlap, devotion—devour. My tooth was dying and small shocks vibrated through the tooth like tiny electrical storms in the Midwest—hail even, a cha-cha-chain-reaction.

The Devil's Workshop

1.

Cock in hand,
heavy and big, too
heavy to hold against gravity's
weight. Large, a whole planet, Mars
maybe, a solar-system orbiting
around my little heart—eight or
nine—age a blur. Little, is all I
can remember, I was little. "Move
it back and forth," Demon
Face commanded me as he stood
over me and I sat on his bed,
"Faster," he said.

I thought, "Matchwood."

He said "Faster!"

I cried "Matchlock!"

but knew he was matador.

I moved my hand
faster.

Sitcom

Mork & Mindy

America

I dream I'm in a 1979 episode. I am Fernando, the plumber.
    I am there to fix the toilet.

In one scene, Mindy writes to Luis Herrera Campíns,
    the president of Venezuela, asking

for human rights. In the next scene, Mork and sixteen Mexicans try
    to cross the border in Arizona.

I shout at them to stop, but they can't hear me. They all die
    in the desert due to heat stroke, dehydration or hyperthermia.

Mork survives, however,
    he's brought back in a spaceship that looks like an egg.

All the others, lost forever in the continuum, or until tomorrow,
    when sixteen more people will try to cross.

This episode is a rerun. In the next scene Mork & Mindy are in McAllen, Texas.
    They're trying to help my friend Miguel and his family

cross the interior border near Brownsville.
    I know this because my tío Rosendo is a coyote and he told me last night.

He's a regular in the show as well. It takes three hours sometimes
to get through the interior checkpoint

of the Rio Grande Valley. Three hours to travel twenty miles!
That's what happens when, in a dream, a court decides

to throw out the Fourth Amendment. A border within
a border, checking the citizenship of Americans traveling through

America and checking for illegal aliens hiding in the tires and gas tanks.
Aliens! Claro que sí in an episode of *Mork*

& Mindy but in gas tanks? Aliens? That's not my language,
but I found those terms

in US immigration law. You can tell a lot about a society
from their public documents.

A whole lot of spaceships and lawbreakers in Texas, Arizona
and California, I guess.

This is why I am thrilled my friend's family appears in this episode.
Rosendo will take them somewhere safe

and not leave them to die in a truck or train like in a different episode when
Mork traveled through time to 2002 and found eight dead people

inside a train car in Denison, Iowa. They
were only trying to get through the interior checkpoint!

This is why I'm glad I've seen this one already.
    Rosendo gets Miguel's family safely through the checkpoint

with an invisible force field that disguises his truck
    and all the alien-ness of it. All the trans-solar-system levers

on the dash with their blinking lights and beam-me-up seats.
    I laugh. I remember how this episode ends.

Rosendo gets Miguel's family safely to Houston where they find work

& blend in fine
    like water or sewage.

America's Bill / La cuenta de América

El precio es un millón de prostitutas en Habana.
El precio es mil de gallones de leche en la boca.
El precio es una primera-dama monolingüe.
El precio es la supremacía blanca y el jefe.
El precio es un muro de frijoles y arroz.
El precio es pelo rubio y manos pequeñas.
El precio es más americanos muertos.
La cuenta siempre llega temprano.
La cuenta nunca llega tarde.

El precio es cincuenta mil de americanos de cara blanca.
El precio es cincuenta mil de antorchas tiki encendidas.
El precio es una cruz encendida.
El precio es un saludo militar erecto.
El precio es mierda de perro en la banqueta.
El precio es mierda de perro en un zapato.
El precio es una americana muerta.
El precio es el llanto destrozado de una madre.
La cuenta siempre llega temprano.
La cuenta nunca llega tarde.

El precio es Portland, Oregon el viernes por la noche.
El precio es un millón de caras anti-Nazi sangrantes.

El precio es meth y supremacistas blancos.
El precio es botellas vacías de vodka.
El precio es una bolsa llena de AR-15s.
El precio es es que no hay pollo en la tienda.
El precio es que no hay alimento para el alma.
El precio es que no comida para el alma.
El precio es un renacimiento espiritual.
El precio es un grupo de tamboreos.
El precio as un tambor rítmico.
El precio es un latido de corazón inexistente.
El precio es la última oración de un pastor.
El precio es el último aliento de un santo.
La cuenta siempre llega temprano.
La cuenta nunca llega tarde.

El precio es un crucero en la bahía de Habana.
El precio es que no hay queso en la tienda cubana.
El precio es la Casa Blanca llena de queso.
El precio es una mierda tupé.
El precio es una cámara de cara anaranjada.
El precio es una ley mierda de infraestructura.
El precio es transportación pública en Cuba.
El precio es el P5 hacia La Rampa.
El precio es La Rampa en la noche.
El precio es una viejita barriendo la calle.
El precio es cinco canales de televisión estatal en Cuba.
El precio es Mirar las hijas en la calle.
El precio es una oración de pollo-muerto.

La cuenta siempre llega temprano.
La cuenta nunca llega tarde.

El precio es fumar un puro.
El precio es la rumba en las calles.
El precio es una isla de grandes poetas.
El precio es un poeta prohibido.
El precio es un poeta prohibido.
El precio es un poeta prohibido.
El precio es jazz de vanguardía.
El precio es una voz hermosa que canta.
El precio es arte en cada esquina.
El precio es música afrocubana.
El precio es la cara de un niño sonriente.
El precio es dinero para la familia.
El precio es la puesta del sol anaranjado.
El precio es nunca dejar la isla.
El precio es un barco de esclavos en el mar..
La cuenta siempre llega temprano.
La cuenta nunca llega tarde.

El precio es América.
El precio es un estado homofóbico.
El precio es desear a más judíos muertos.
El precio quiere más mexicanos muertos.
El precio La cuenta quiere un esclavo en la hoguera.
El precio es América ahorita.
El precio es América el año anterior.

El precio es cien lenguas distintas.
El precio es una boca muy abierta de par en par.
El precio es un millón de pies abiertos.
El precio es una panocha llena de trampa.
El precio es mil galones de leche por la garganta.
El precio es la comida de panocha de la ducha.
El precio es es un cura perdido orando.
El precio es una mano tambor-del-mar.
El precio es el tiempo mismo.
El precio siempre conoce tu nombre.
El precio es muy muy largo.
La cuenta
La cuenta
La cuenta
es siempre más de lo que se puede pagar.

The Devil's Workshop

1.
Lo.

Demon Face a pedo-mosaic-phile of many one single experienced moments. Demon Face, a camper parked outside a house. Demon Face, the shower at the basketball court. Demon Face behind a dirt hill, as we three-wheeled, at Walt Disney World—in my bathroom in Moses Lake—in his basement in outer-space—in my sleep—in the beauty of the sky—in the clouds. Demon Face as I dream—in my pee—when I leche—at school—during lunch—in my mouth—on the bed—below the sheets—in a car—on the hike—in a canoe—after the run—before the dinner—after we play—during church—in the hymn—over the mountain ridge.

LO

1.

Can you remember the first time
you came?
    Remember
    who
    you
    were
    with? I remember it
was the holidays, I used to cum a
lot during the holidays.
    Remember how it felt
like it was a punch
    to the pucker?
        Remember
how it felt
        like a punch
        when
        you
        came
        in the pucker?

I remember
I used
to be alive.
The first time
I
came
I was
eight.
I
remember   I used
to be alive.
I
remember wondering what it
was going to feel like
the first time   I
came.
A bluebird?

Or   tiny
blue
balls
bloo-
burd?

And when I finally came,
the thing that surprised me the most

was when

/ Lo / pulled / back / my cousin's face

/ Lo /

jacked me off

/ his eyes / some other island /

/ Demon Face / Some other island /

the coast of a tongue. /

Lo

1.

Pig, I

wanted

to call

him /

Demon

Face. /

P

I

G

I

wanted to call

the rotten

three-

wheeler

and

the

awful

man-sized

mayO

spread

picnic sandwiches that we
always [packed].
Pig I wanted to call me,

me,

me,

most of all.

P

I

G

G

I

P

P I

G

Gee

I Pee

with

his

hands

all

Ov-

er

me.

Un

-der

Me.

Beside   me.

~~Thro~~

~~ugh~~

me.

A-

part

from

me.

Could never

hol-

d

me.

Always

b-

r-

o-

k-e

me.

Never

tried

to

fix

me.

Or

s-

orry

me.

In

the

family

of

me.

From the

Boardwalk

in Havana.

You, the tourist, approach by air above the bay like a voyeuristic
angel & the Malecón & the buildings of El Centro

Havana establish where you are; the rubble & ruin—
could be a beat-up Atlantic City, but it is not.

You, the tourist, glide like a child's
paper plane, one foot above the bay, & notice the 1559

Spanish fortress Castillo de la Real Fuerza, built to protect
Spain's investment. This is where the reaping

of humans & gold was stored before heading back across
the ocean. You smile as waves lap

& crack shore-rock then turn
in on each other & flip around like a graceful Olympic

swimmer. "Cool," says the wind as it exits left,
over the Malecón's edge & into the water where rock formations

look like broken dock-piers that once held boats closer than a tourist's
wallet. You settle in on a street corner in Centro Havana.

You stand outside a hustle shop scam.
Someone needs milk for their dying baby. Some

other one just needs two pesos to buy diapers. A woman
wearing a light blue wrap on her head crosses

your path from the right. You notice black & grey hair growing
on her chin, like miniature palm trees in the wind. One hair sways

& she smiles as she stares at something further than you can see.
You, the drained tourist, the babbling bleached body in the sun,

you go inside a corner store that wants to sell you
some flowering coming-of-age,

only you don't want to buy any coming-of-age, so you tell the man no, but
thank you & in a really nice voice. He laughs when you tell him no.

A group of young boys enter the store & ask you for money, you say no again.
Their skin black & more beautiful than a shiny piece of tar heroin

that entombs ten years worse than a slammed gavel.
You, the converted socialist. You, the Che Guevara-hat-wearing

chummy-chum-chum & these kids want something from you,
want something more than you can give.

Don't be afraid to partake in the Santeria
chop-a-head-off-a-chicken dinner,

& the Rumba in the street goes
boom, boom, boom. How about a nice

heirloom for the kids? One boy asks
for a peso; two girls ask for two.

The sky, bluer than the '63 Chevy that just passed
outside as you shout no, no, no & the jackhammer

goes trr, trrr, trrrrr over the whistle of girls.
Over the fifty gallons of water for just one flush,

over the collapse of the Soviet sickle crush
& just when you are about to give up on this place, a giant & long palm

tree of a silhouetted boy takes up the whole left side
of the frame he entered from. He is taller than the Christ-by-the-bay

Statue! He is blocking all of the sun & is darker than the asphalt
of the People's Communist Square!

He winks as his watch falls off his wrist
as he runs past you into the street, crossing lanes of traffic

like a kickoff return & you run after him, shouting, "Son, your watch,
son, you dropped your watch." But you are too slow & the young man

is getting away like a launched shuttle, like someone about to leave this earth.
All you can do is think of the children swimming on the other side of the

Malecón's edge this boy is running towards. The ones swimming
in the dirty water below, the cement that looks like urban coral reefs

that will crush him. You can't see any way he is going to make it over
the crumbling mock pier and not crack his head open

right in front of your eyes. But this boy is running with the speed.
So fast the pesos in his pocket start to spin & make

a Mario Bros *ching, ching, ching, ching* sound as he leaps off the top
of the Malecón & out into the bay like a bomb exploding at the feet

of a little girl. Like an equation on the board sparking chalk
into dust & the boy does it, he clears the jump,

clears everyone lying on the rocks below
& the rocks themselves, the boy Jesse Owenses the leap,

the leap exploding beyond heat & humidity,
all of this fear, beyond everything Cold War & Revolutionary & you,

the pot-bellied tourist, do the only thing that's right,
you open your wallet to him like a caught fish

split up the belly, heart
& blood rushing out.

Harrowing of Hell
666.

I was being baptized away from the undead. Mother of Mary now and forever's flame on my cheek. A spirit of perversion roared up in me. "Mother may I feel Mary," I said. Then I heard music, seven trumpets playing.

"Mom, why is it burning?" *Hold still Mijo*,
she said to me. My mother,
standing only four feet eleven, was
locked onto some spirit. My mom asked,

Do you believe

in the Holy Spirit,

the holy Catholic

Church,

the communion

of saints?

"I do," I said,

but I

didn't.

She

slowly started moving

her hand up the side of

my cheek like she was shaving me.

She had the spirit in her hand—

Beelzebub,

red and hot,

the spirit of Death

and Decay caught

in her hand

and

moving

up

my cheek

like a shackled

prisoner. My mother

commanded,

Baal, Spirit of Death

and Decay, I remove you now, in the name

of the lamb,

and a burn like

a rocket launch glowed from within my

head.

My mother whispered close to my ear

a lullaby.

I could feel

a body of some mass

of some sort

coming out of me—sonnets

of the flesh—a dusty cloud

of moist particles—heavy,

but not seen.

We rested for a while.

Anaphora, chiasmus, diacope, polyptoton

Rhetorical Figures & a Bullet

crossing the border.

My brothers and sisters are dying in train cars. Overcome
by one-hundred-degree days, my brothers

and sisters die. They are carried like cargo
along Interstate 8 in the trunks of automobiles

as American as piñatas in the aisles of Walmart in rural towns
across the Midwest. My brothers and sisters are carrying

the weight of return tickets to Mexico, Cuba, Guatemala,
Nicaragua, Honduras, El Salvador. They need us to care.

My brothers and sisters are being shot at
in Mexico while thinking of crossing the border in San Ysidro,

named for the patron saint of farmers near San Diego.
My brothers and sisters are bleeding to death

from gunshot wounds by American border patrol agents
in El Paso, Texas. They have bled

from chest wounds, from shoulder wounds, from leg wounds,
from wounds left open, my brothers and sisters bleed.

On June 8, 2010, a fifteen-year-old Mexican citizen
was shot to death on the Mexican side of the border near El Paso.

Passport stampless! Bullets, bullets! Passport stampless!

Rumba,

Chango &

A Singular Moment

How many hawks

circle in the heat

of heart-break?

A santero in the street   red & white

guts. A dog is tearing

through   the skin & bones of

a fish. Three dumpsters

in the center of centro

Havana. Daddy Yankee,

Pitbull's "Gasolina"

shaking every window second-floor dance.

How much rum

can one person drink? A gallon

is a shark in the ocean.

One CUC   two CUC   all the fish caught

in a day.

O mar   O mar

Omar   a drunk in the street

throws out all the leche

in the evening.

The

Devil's Workshop

1.

I started to earthquake. The hit I shot in my arm was Grand Canyon and airplane jump!

Demon Face and Ghost Scream. The hit was nonpartisan and nonprofit—What is this nonsense? "How could this be nonprofit," I thought. "This at least has to be QAnon!"

My body shaking violently. I grabbed onto the two sides of the white bathroom sink and started to zipper. I thought for sure my heart was going to pop. QAnon!

Capitalism! For profit! My heart-cash-rate bank account soaring! Investments too! The NASDAQ over 30,000! I was holding on for life—shirtless, shoeless, bending

at my knees,

breathing in and out of my mouth like I was giving myself CPR, trying to slow everything down around me—to not Slipknot.

"Just survive the hit," my drool said as it hit the dry-blood brown carpet floor—the walls around me vibrating like a Heimlich maneuver of sound or sunlight—my own brain too, genus of addiction, in heliotrope—wobbling back and forth—erect to the sun, underneath my yellow tetanus sunken eye sockets—there it was, my demon face.

"Mom, mother, manteca" I shouted again. "Hold me close." My two hands ready to rip the bathroom sink right off the wall—breathe in, breathe out—the quake wasn't slowing down—I wasn't going to make it. I looked up at the bathroom mirror again and looked into my demon face—a tiny wounded rabbit. I blinked my eyes and the glaucoma-glazed-demon-eyes were gone, and my heartbeat began to slow.

A roller-bandage sale. A rolling-pin to the head. A romantic romp. A roofless home. A rookie in the room of hanging rope.

Letter

To Stafford from la Frontera

del Columbia Basin

ACT 1, Action 1.

(Fuego's Anagram Chorus' Eulogy for *BRACHYLAGUS IDAHOENSIS* and the American Farmer

OUTLOUD ONLY! And as many times as needed, and in a rocking motion).

A Baa

Decrying Shush Soil

A Baa

Hunched Glossy Iris

A Baa

Descrying Shush Oil

A Baa

Descrying Hush Silo

A Baa

Descrying Hush Oils

A Baa

Descrying Hush Soil

A Baa

Decrying Shush Silo

A Baa Decrying Shush Soil
A Baa Hunched Glossy Iris
A Baa Descrying Shush Oil
A Baa Decrying Shush Silo

A Baa Descrying Hush Silo
A Baa Descrying Hush Oils
A Baa Descrying Hush Soil

A Baa Decrying Shush Oils
A Baa Chloride Gushy Sins
A Baa Decrying Shush Soil

A Baa Decrying Hush Silos
A Baa Chide Hurlings Soys
A Baa Chide Shrugs Nosily
A Baa Lynched Soughs Iris
A Baa Lurched Hissing Soy

A Baa Children Sighs Yous
A Baa Chloride Gushy Sins
A Baa Lynched Roguish Sis

ACT 2.

(fast and clapping)

BRACHYLAGUS IDAHOENSIS.

Plans for recommendation and

recovery: @

~~best available information~~, Fox-Con-Roger-Ailes-pant-drop, climate change isn't real!

BRACHYLAGUS

IDAHOENSIS.

BRACHYLAGUS IDAHOENSIS.

BRACHYLAGUS IDAHOENSIS.

BRACHYLAGUS IDAHOENSIS.

Listed as threatened or endangered pursuant

to

the

Endangered

Species

Act

of

1973,

as

amended. (stop clapping).

—a flute end of

consequences Stafford once wrote.

Chorus sings, fuego fuego fuego.

Dear Bill, I write to you

from La Frontera del Columbia Basin.

A geographically isolated and genetically distinct population of... American farmers.

QBadgers, Bill, found in Washington State.

Pygmy rabbits are herbivores found in the sagebrush ecosystem. They serve as prey for

weasels, coyotes, badgers, bobcats, raptors, owls, ravens, crows, and foxes!

Ravens wind-born western and somersaults the river

habitats.

Habitats, pygmy rabbit burrows

sagebrush country. QBadgers Bill!

Fuego fuego fuego.

ACT 3, Action 1.

Dear Bill, I write to you

from La Frontera del Columbia Basin.

A geographically isolated and genetically distinct population of weasel-deplorables!

Enemy to the pygmy, BIPOC, LGBTQ+, +All WOMEN.

Burrows deep, blood. Loose fox soil, kin and kindle, Kittitas Valley generations—
Valley View Elementary and Morgan Middle school—horses and children

to avoid (said fast) Pedophile

Pedophile

Pedophile

Pedophile!

Many other species use pygmy rabbit burrows, including black-tailed jackrabbits, least chipmunks, and mountain cottontails.

Dear Bill, I write to

you from La Frontera del Columbia Basin

A geographically isolated and genetically distinct population of Ravens, and QAnonowls! The rural American farmer Bill—traitor to the earth and dark soil, soy-traitor to the constitution and good neighbors.

Dear Bill, I write to you

from ACT 3, Action 2.

(To be read fast and aloud-or until mouth stops moving)

Fuego fuego fuego. Fuego fuego fuego fuego fuego fuego. Fuego fuego fuego fuego. Fuego fuego fuego. Fuego fuego fuego fuego fuego fuego. Fuego fuego fuego fuego. Fuego fuego fuego. Fuego fuego fuego fuego fuego fuego. Fuego fuego fuego fuego. Fuego fuego fuego. Fuego fuego fuego fuego fuego fuego. Fuego fuego fuego fuego. Fuego fuego fuego. Fuego fuego fuego fuego fuego fuego. Fuego fuego fuego fuego. Fuego fuego fuego. Fuego fuego fuego fuego fuego fuego. Fuego fuego fuego fuego. Fuego fuego fuego. Fuego fuego fuego fuego fuego fuego. Fuego fuego fuego fuego. Fuego fuego fuego. Fuego fuego fuego fuego fuego fuego. Fuego fuego fuego fuego. Fuego fuego fuego. Fuego fuego fuego fuego fuego fuego. Fuego fuego fuego fuego. Fuego fuego fuego. Fuego fuego fuego fuego fuego fuego. Fuego fuego fuego fuego. Fuego fuego fuego. Fuego fuego fuego fuego fuego fuego. Fuego fuego fuego fuego. Fuego fuego fuego. Fuego fuego fuego fuego fuego fuego. Fuego fuego fuego fuego. Fuego fuego fuego. Fuego fuego fuego fuego fuego fuego. Fuego fuego fuego fuego. Fuego fuego fuego. Fuego fuego fuego fuego fuego fuego. Fuego fuego fuego fuego. Fuego fuego fuego. Fuego fuego fuego fuego fuego fuego. Fuego fuego fuego fuego. Fuego fuego fuego. Fuego fuego fuego fuego fuego fuego. Fuego fuego fuego fuego. Fuego fuego fuego. Fuego fuego fuego fuego fuego fuego. Fuego fuego fuego fuego. Fuego fuego fuego. Fuego fuego fuego fuego fuego fuego. Fuego fuego fuego fuego. Fuego fuego fuego. Fuego fuego fuego fuego fuego fuego. Fuego fuego fuego fuego. Fuego fuego fuego. Fuego fuego fuego fuego fuego fuego. Fuego fuego fuego fuego. Fuego fuego fuego. Fuego fuego fuego fuego fuego fuego. Fuego fuego fuego fuego. Fuego fuego fuego. Fuego fuego fuego fuego fuego fuego. Fuego fuego fuego fuego. Fuego fuego fuego. Fuego fuego fuego fuego fuego fuego. Fuego fuego fuego fuego.

ACT 4.

More fuego.

Dear Bill, I write to you from La

Frontera del Columbia Basin

A geographically isolated and genetically distinct population of baby-eating Trump-raptors, and pedophile foxes! Enemy to the pygmy! Enemy to DEMOCRACY!

Fuego fuego fuego DEMOCRACY, Bill!
Trump-raptors, Qfoxes, and pedophile owl-traitors—
American terrorists! January 6th Mob rules!

Dear Bill, I write to

you from La Frontera del Columbia Basin

A geographically isolated and genetically distinct population of supporters of QLies. The death of apple pie Bill! No more nature poetry readings! Did you know Hillary Clinton eats red-blood-baby-sushi California rolls and trolls!

Charlie Manson's prison jack sock on eBay!
Fuego! Comet Pizza!
Fuego! Baby-eating NBA players!
Fuego! January 6th domestic terrorism day! No school forever!
Raptors, Trump-traitors, and Qfoxes!

Dear Bill, I write.

Alphabet's annunciations and advice to

Barack Obama

after watching him take the oath

Adam, Eve or Abel never liked a tiny American noun like fear dressed up Black or black &
white like a teeny-weeny tinseled Christmas tree Kenyan son of an intellectual
eyeglass black-rimmed colonized man.

Brother O's mama's blanket folded like an African omelet of elegant Swahili & Uncle
Sammy-Sam-Sam Hawaiian-English pineapples & ham.

Copper Canyon Press never copyrighted the Jamestown, 1611, Cornflower Cornucopia
by Cornet corn-fed-slave owner Jefferson. Corny I know, but ain't no Major
Jackson poetry on the shelves of the Seattle Public Library, "Must be all
checked out!"

D is for Dantrell Davis & for all of the people, places, & things that have, like the
Donahue show, died & where I first learned about Cabrini-Green housing &
tag-toe Gangster Disciple reaper boys or $10 Washington Ave reefer bags.

E is for Egypt & the epiphany that every dog has its day. Jeremiah Wright was right!
America's chickens are coming home to roost. Tribeca to Trinity Church the sun
breathes eight years' presidential neglect.

Fudge or a vanilla-sprinkled top? F@$k Saddle-back ranch Rick Warren can't
even dance, looks too much like Rush Limbaugh popping pills to be my
metaphysical religious grand poo-bah.

Gorgeous hanging-tree Georgetown girls study the GRE & eat chocolate ice cream
on the great George Washington lawn. Genghis Khan. Louis Farrakhan.

Harryette Mullen's lyrical mathematical mayhem may be able to save the world
banks, please captain prez, just no more bear-market military tanks.

I ain't no Mexican Colonel Sanders creamy-cream-cream pickled
coleslaw pretending to write poetry under a starry-starry
you-know-who night.

Jaw broke. Jaw jacked. Jackass. GOP John.

Kill bill number three; pass bill Emily-XYZ, no more JFK presidential Dallas drive-by talk,
hush.

Live & the lithosphere says watch out for the rope's loop splinters.

Mud & the Black vote says get up, run, don't be dumb, don't get hit or delayed by any
Uncle Tom-Tom sunny-sun-son-Washington solar bombs, don't get caught in the
"W" house wearing a blouse or a thong. "All I said was don't get caught."

N is for the fourteenth letter in the English alphabet, birthed in the Congo,
transported in a slave ship, knocked down like bowling-ball pins in
Chicago, New Orleans, Atlanta & Los Angeles. The letter was beheaded
on MTV & in the inner city by bling.

Obama went to Harvard, studied books & crooks, learned to move Bishop
diagonal, stand tall like a chessboard rook-
ie & the slave-ship owners' chorus laments *this is not exactly how we look.*

P-l-e-a-s-e quit &

Quayle all of your Martha's Vineyard
    wine & cheese. Bitchin'

Recession wouldn't you say? & the slave-ship
    owners' chorus

Says *put your finger in your okey-dokey, poo-poo-pokey*

Transatlantic son of a Kansas-Hawaiian bell. We come equipped with

Ugly. I beg you, America's faithful lyric, unbuckle the shackles from around your tight-
    formed half 'n' half hips, ain't nothing polyester about Barack or Bobama the dog.

Vacancy filled! No need for any Alaska to drill. No apologies, Mr. Obama, I know you
    are not a direct descendant of slaves but symbolically, holler!

Whoa, whoa, woe. Wag your tail & say hello to your new Sí, se puede immigration border
    swine flu hell.

Xerox any documents that say you are our 44th president and that you won a second term.

Yak, yak, yak, all the way to college speaking engagements. Yelp when you see the dollar
    against the yen & definitely, definitely, definitely,

Zero out the chorus of the zombie-slave-ship owners' hearts who can still be heard
    zigzagging the grave-filled Atlantic:

this is not exactly how
we look, this is not
what we intended,

this is not what we shackled in the huge hulls of our ships.

R.I.P. Hoodie dreaming in the afterlife

Sanford, Florida

7-13-13 late

"Emmanuel, Emmanuel," Hoodie says as he stumbles through a Washington forest.
"Fuck this shit!" Fence shouts & jumps over the edge of Snoqualmie waterfall

as if Fence was late for a party. *The body of a young boy*, rushing water over a fall,
all beauty as mist lifts into air from contact. Fence said, "I told you so!

What did you expect! What did you think was going to happen?" The Cradle of Cambridge!
"Magdalen, Magdalen, *am I forgotten*?" Hoodie cries. "I thought I had a chance!"

The forest's chorus sings, *As mist lifts into air from contact.* "Trinity, Trinity," Hoodie shouts!
"Trinity, Trinity, where are your studied halls? Where is your branch of knowledge?"

"Chance!" Fence screams. "Chance? Oh, like the chances my homies have
of-not-going-to-jail after a speeding ticket in Arizona's SB 1070 a.k.a. send a homie to jail

chance? I like your odds!" exclaims Fence. Hoodie yells, "But I'm only seventeen!"
Hoodie knew he needed to get to the ocean so Hoodie followed the Snoqualmie River

down & out into Puget Sound. The forest's chorus sings,
The sun setting like this verdict, as mist lifts into air from contact.

Fence was getting nervous, told Hoodie, "I don't know how to swim."
Hoodie told Fence *not to worry*, that Hoodie knew water well.

"An ocean of history," Hoodie said. "Do you know *Gorée Island*?
The water there, dark & blue as a three-day-cut umbilical cord.

Palm trees silhouette the haze—*Saint-Louis! Saint-Louis! Saint-Louis!*—
rock me to sleep in your water. *Senegal! Cambridge!*

Where are my Quaker brothers, who will and will not own me?
Where are their voting ways?

The fringe of Kent! Kill me some Indians! Buy me some slaves! Rape me some
women! The forest's chorus signs, *They are my hands, my workers, my people.*

Goree Island? Saint-Louis! The sun setting like this verdict, as mist lifts into air
from contact. They are my hands, my workers, my people. Cambridge, not to worry.

Hoodie got lost in all the islands in Puget Sound. Fence was scared and holding onto Hoodie tight. The weight of Fence started to sink both Fence and Hoodie.

A *Chinook* Salmon grabbed Hoodie by the hood and pulled Hoodie and Fence
back up to the top of the water. Fence was crying, "I want to go back to Land.

The dry heat of the dirt, my friend, even if I'm caged by who I am."
Chinook Salmon says, "Caged by who you are? Deep!

You can't go back to land. THEY will kill you! THEY will kill you!
They killed all of my family. The *Tlingit, Nisga'a, Tsetsaut, Haida, Tsimshian, Gitxsan, Haisla,*

Heiltsuk, Wuikinuxv, Kwakwaka'wakw, Nuu-chah-nulth, Makah, Coast Salish, Nuxálk, Willapa,
Chimakum, and the *Quileute*! Everyone is dead but me. You cannot stay here.

I will show you your way out." Salmon looked scared but continued, "Follow the North Pacific
current down to South America, once you get there, jump onto the North Equatorial current

until you get through the Indonesian Islands—a thread going through a needle.
Connect with the South Equatorial to the Mozambique current.

That current will pull you down to the bottom of Africa
As if you were a drowning child, when you get there be sure to jump

onto the Benguela current right into Saint-Louis, Senegal."
"Emmanuel, Magdalen, Trinity, where are your studied halls?

How your living-heart baffles me," Hoodie yells as Hoodie drifts with Fence
on a piece of wood down and out towards California, orcas giving them their last push

southward. Fence mutters, "Who makes all this stuff up? Wish I had some *hors d'oeuvres.*"
"Fuck the uncut French," North Pacific current says. "They need deodorant!"

Hoodie shouts, "How about some *lo mein*?"
"Hell yes!" Fence says!

My people! North Pacific current sang, *My people!*
And so it was all the way to Saint-Louis, Senegal.

North Pacific current sang, *My people! My people!*
All my beautiful-beautiful brown and black and tan

people. All, all and always my people.
Waves rocked them back and forth.

Nosotros

PATRIOT

Americans

When the nipple of a mother's breast
fills my mouth

with milk and I am waterboarded to near death—my broken
limbs ragged with

blood and my crimson gravel leg snaps
the concrete street

& sun bakes
a sister, a mother, a father—to a friend blown into pieces.

When you, the passive American tourist, have your child
lowered onto a Judas

chair & your child's rectum engulfs
a wooden triangle point like a chestnut being pried open

& ghostly white patriots pry false truths from your child's dry cracked mouth &
there in the windowless room

your child's anus shiny like a baby's crowning head, bleeds with olive oil,
        bleeds with lost dreams

        bleeds with chains tied to a ceiling &
a barking dog.

When the nipple of a breast of a mother is pulled from my mouth & a pear
                                                                                                                                        of anguish

is shoved in, right after, breaking all of my teeth & the fragments of pulp
                                                                                                        fragments of dentin

                                                                                                                            of enamel
                                                                                                                            & cementum

are stepped on by patriotic men and a tiny tooth fragment
penetrates a strong desert tan boot

& shoots up directly into the nervous system
of an operative—

                                                                                                                    into
                                                                                                                    the innermost portion

of a soul
of a connective tissue

of nerves

& blood vessels that nourish patriotism.

When all gods are dead & Allah means the same as Christ on the Cross
& Christ on the Cross means the same as detonation—

means the same as blood kit
blood in a bag & a mosque—

means a child's dangling ankle & a brown child's face hooded like Trayvon in a casket—
into biohazard bags, *into father forgive them*—

into the rotation of a crime scene compass &
a faint traced body barely seen in a thousand bits of a brutal explosion—

means a consent-to-search form &
all relatives are going to prison—means *for they know not what they do.*

Means drawing logs substitute for a whole body
that once was—*amen I say to thee.*

Then, somewhere, there, all over in dried bits in the
bend
of a concrete curb in prayer, a dead body's soul

praying Allah & Christ quenched throat &   we are patriots you & I.

We are, together the plural passive American terrorist,

we are measuring up in numbers
at the national forensic mapping station—*this day thou shalt be with me in paradise*

at the
Valley View elementary school assembly

in Ellensburg, Washington— at the
Sunday, Christ on the Cross gathering

on Chestnut Street & in the Four Square Church— at the
annual Central Washington University Native Pow Wow & salmon feed—

at the
Mission Ridge ski slope in Wenatchee, Washington where we bomb down the mountain

on Sunday mornings on snowboards & explode off jumps, then we pray before lunch.

Behold thy mother. My God, my God, why hast thou forsaken me?
We are good Sunday bombers—

passive American terrorists

bombing the ridge in the sun

& late in the afternoon.
We are patriot terrorist hiding

in the aisles of a Trader Joe's &
we are healthy Americans, you & I—*I thirst.*

It is consummated. We are the alpha & the omega—*into thy hands*
I command my spirit &

at night, just after prayer
we are feeding our hungry

crying-out children
every last God-damn thing they need.

Harrowing of Hell

666.

Aflame my body tingled, wanted

to float. A powerless powerline.

I saw my reflection—a

wilderness in a wolf.

El spirit y Lo.

My head cocked

back as far as a howl.

My back

completely

bent.

I let out

another burst of air—a chorus of

wolves in concert.

My mother moved

her Bible up the outside of
my throat and over my face.
Prayer, pray, and preach.

I felt

a mass

of something

rising from inside my
throat—a slow snaking tsunami.

My tiny mother spoke

and pressed her Bible
onto my chest, a power station, a
power hammer, a power shovel, a
power
house

and suspended

me

in

midair.

Baal,

Spirit of Lust and

Perversion,

I command you to

leave—Demon Face Jezebel,

Bathsheba! And again,

in tongues, spoke,

Shubadha, Nicarra,

Ruskadha,

I the holy in spirit. I AM.

The holy

believe in the church. I tried to

outrun the words, this out-of-the-

world deliverance. She continued,

I am the root and the offspring

of David

Ruskadha, Nicarra,

Shubadha.

"Merciful madre! conquistadora!

what is happening to me?"

I shouted as I floated

in space.

My limbs,

electrical wires sparking light in all

of the house.

The house aglow.

The house aflame.

My mother the magician—aglow

like a lamp.

A lamp

like a flame.

Then her

voice illuminated the sky,

my body

amplified and released

from

the

air

and fell flat on my back,

bruised

and beaten. My

mother's nipple-milk voice spoke

but no voice was heard,

only light and in

that light

a bolt of

sound and I

heard light, and in

that sound

the ravished

spirits of Satan's minions

whimpered and released

me when the light spoke,

"Spirits

I command you.

With the lamb,

I consume the wolf—*behold, come*

hither."

The Devil's Workshop

1.

Each tattoo and injection tried to flatline Demon Face, to delete me from that little truck camper where the summer squash happened. The naked mermaid on my arm, the eight ball with a sailor hat on top of it, two scorpions pinching, the number thirteen, a red rose, the big apple, a cherry bomb, a skull apple for NYC and the Latin King who got thrown off the roof top in alphabet city. Demon Face—Seattle's Space Needle, sumo wrestler Takanohana, Saint Sabrina's cross-halo symbol, praying hands and my dead dogs' names on my fingers. Demon Face—a horseshoe, a dollar bill sign with the words "NITE, NITE" on my knuckles. Demon Face—eight years of eight-balls. Demon Face "FTW" across my stomach and a huge dragon on my back. The word "GRACE" on the inside of my mouth's lip. "CRACKED OUT," on my chest. I remember Demon Face saying, "Hey, you want to see something cool?" And that's how it happened, to see "something cool?"

"What are you doing," I asked and started to move toward the door. "Wait, wait," Demon Face said and grabbed me like I was a small animal. His hands rabies and rabid, keeping me there, in the bathroom—a caged rabbit. "Wait, watch, something is going to happen," Demon Face tilted his head back toward the ceiling of the bathroom like he was seeing God and let out a small moan as white, sticky, stigmata-stuff came out.

The stigmata got all over the bathtub.

"*The world is a wolf.* His hot breath at the keyhole,
his terrible threats—let him wait."

—Katharine Whitcomb

ACKNOWLEDGMENTS

Many of these poems first appeared in the chapbook *Barbarian at the Gate*, published by the Poetry Society of America. "Nosotros PATRIOT Americans" first appeared under a different title in *The Rumpus*.

Much love to A Gathering of Tribes "Stoop" Workshop, Nuyorican Poets Cafe, and the Canons of East Third Street: (R.I.P) Miguel Algarín, (R.I.P) Steve Cannon, and Bob Holman. Their mentorship shapes the face of twenty-first century literature.

Thanks to the smoking J's of Ellensburg, WA: Jampa Dorje, Jane Orleman, Maya Jewell Zeller, Jen Lynn, and Joanna Thomas for their artistic lifeblood.

Much gratitude to my family at Poetry Northwest, Humanities Washington, Iowa State University MFA, and in the English Department at Central Washington University.

Wendy Barnes, Ava Chin, Dan Martin, Christopher Schedler, Crystal Williams, and Josh Welsh for their professional support.

Extra big thanks to Cleveland State University Poetry Center's Caryl Pagel, Zach Peckham, and Hilary Plum for believing in this book and to Sevy Perez for design. You all are so beautiful.

René V. Baca, and Nathalie Kasselis for their Spanish edits.

Editorial thanks to Wendy Barnes, Caryl Pagel, and Connor L. Simons for their brilliant vision.

Thanks to CA Conrad, Jennifer L. Knox, Lucas De Lima, Willie Perdomo, and Edwin Torres for your kind words on the back of this book.

Eduardo C. Corral and Katharine Whitcomb for their opening and closing quotes in this book.

Karla Maravilla, my poetic daughter and co-conspirator in performance. Keep knocking.

My children: Brooklyn, Carlos and Dominic Cavazos: that's my heart right there!

photo courtesy of Dean Davis

Xavier Cavazos is a performance artist and a grand slam champion of the Nuyorican Poets Cafe in NYC, and a member of three national poetry slam teams. He is the author of three award-winning poetry collections: *Barbarian at the Gate* (Poetry Society of America), *Diamond Grove Slave Tree* (Ice Cube Press), and *The Devil's Workshop* (editor's choice selection from the Cleveland State University Poetry Center). Currently, Cavazos is a senior poetry editor for *Poetry Northwest*, directs the Liberal Studies Program at Central Washington University, and serves on the board of trustees for Humanities Washington.

RECENT CLEVELAND STATE UNIVERSITY POETRY CENTER PUBLICATIONS

edited by Caryl Pagel & Hilary Plum

POETRY

World'd Too Much: The Selected Poetry of Russell Atkins
ed. Kevin Prufer and Robert E. McDonough

Advantages of Being Evergreen by Oliver Baez Bendorf

Dream Boat by Shelley Feller

My Fault by Leora Fridman

Orient by Nicholas Gulig

Twice There Was A Country by Alen Hamza

Age of Glass by Anna Maria Hong

outside voices, please by Valerie Hsiung

In One Form to Find Another by Jane Lewty

50 Water Dreams by Siwar Masannat

Mule: 10th Anniversary Edition by Shane McCrae

daughterrarium by Sheila McMullin

The Bees Make Money in the Lion by Lo Kwa Mei-en

Residuum by Martin Rock

Festival by Broc Rossell

Sun Cycle by Anne Lesley Selcer

Arena by Lauren Shapiro

Bottle the Bottles the Bottles the Bottles by Lee Upton

Innocence by Michael Joseph Walsh

No Doubt I Will Return A Different Man by Tobias Wray

ESSAYS

I Liked You Better Before I Knew You So Well
by James Allen Hall

A Bestiary by Lily Hoang

Codependence by Amy Long

Telephone: Essays in Two Voices
by Brenda Miller and Julie Marie Wade

The Leftovers by Shaelyn Smith

TRANSLATIONS

Almost Obscene by Raúl Gómez Jattin,
translated by Katherine M. Hedeen and Olivia Lott

Scorpionic Sun by Mohammed Khaïr-Eddine,
translated by Conor Bracken

I Burned at the Feast: Selected Poems of Arseny Tarkovsky,
translated by Philip Metres and Dimitri Psurtsev

for a complete list of titles visit CSUPoetryCenter.com